SILICON VALLEY

A WAY THROUGH

Silicon Valley

A Way Through

**The mindset behind
the world's largest innovation
and technology cluster.**

By Felipe Lamounier

ISBN-13: 978-1-7028121-1-5

Cover design and layout by UPSampa
Cover design © UPSampa
Edited by Marissa Waraksa @mariesa_faer

Printed in the United States of America

I dedicate this book to my family.
For the formation of my character; for the protection
and safe driving, at all times of my life.
To Marcela, specifically, for being the biggest
encourager of my dreams.
Her support has helped me overcome the days of
discouragement and tiredness.

I dedicate this book, as well, to all those
who have always believed in and supported me.
Thank you.

*"There's no single right place to be an entrepreneur,
but certainly there's something about Silicon Valley."*

— Peter Thiel

Author's Note

We are living in a world that changes at a rate much faster than ever before, and as a result, people and companies are realizing how they are becoming obsolete much faster as well (the feeling of "FOMO" — Fear of Missing Out). Thus, so many feel they have a continual and urgent demand to keep up with the innovation and learning disruptions that appear each and every day.

This book was written to share with readers the mindset behind, and what can be learned from, the world's largest innovation and technology cluster, as it has been transforming and impacting the way we relate, do business, communicate and live in society for over the last five decades.

ACKNOWLEDGMENTS

This book would not exist without the support of many people.

Firstly, I would like to express my sincere thanks to my friend and partner Mauricio Benvenutti, for planting the seed of this book, for sharing this journey in Silicon Valley with me, and for his generosity and inspiration.

To my friend Tommaso di Bartolo, who gave me the final push to share what I've learned in Silicon Valley with the world. Much of what I know about Silicon Valley, I have had the opportunity to learn from him.

To Fernando Toti and the UPSampa team, for taking care of the entire design of this book. You guys rock crazily!

To my great friend Ercy Gomes, for being a great promoter and supporter of my work.

To my StartSe team, for sharing this dream together. What we have built so far together has been amazing and the most amazing thing is knowing what lies ahead!

Believing that it is possible to build on your own is to deceive yourself. I thank all those who directly and indirectly contributed along the way so that I could get here.

CONTENTS

ANGELIKA BLENDSTRUP

Thursday night in San Francisco and the room is buzzing with the voices of 100 international entrepreneurs, all here in Silicon Valley full of anticipation as they expect to get a deep look into what it takes to create a startup. They are the new attendees of a current StartSe Immersive Program in Silicon Valley and are participating in an intensive week-long transformation that will send them back to Brazil with minds and hearts opened to new ideas and ventures.

At the center of it all is StartSe, setting the world of Latin American entrepreneurs on fire. Felipe Lamounier, specifically, stands as one of the torchbearers lighting it.

Felipe has added writing this book to all the responsibilities he has taken over, all because he is so passionate about telling others what he has had to learn while going through making StartSe, the company, along with its programs here in Silicon Valley, successful in this special environment.

It is his intent to share the knowledge of what it took to build this venture by addressing international professionals, in the hopes that they will benefit from his experiences and insights, and can then turn his gleanings into successes of their own.

Felipe himself has been an entrepreneur in Silicon Valley for the past five years, and has jumped in with both feet to learn the "secrets" of the Valley; e.g., how to create valuable networks, what it takes to genuinely connect with others, and how to build companies, projects and products here.

In ten chapters, some of the topics Felipe discusses are: how to build a great team, how to build a product with a focus on quick execution and intensity, why lifelong learning is so essential in the 21st century, and he closes with "give back to society", the philosophy on which much of SV is built.

How do I know Felipe? I've been in Silicon Valley for 20 years and work with international entrepreneurs [including 500 Startups and Singularity University Labs], mentoring them to help fulfill their dreams — something which gives me a great sense of accomplishment in my own life [and keeps me on the pulse of what's new]. In addition, as a

Venture Partner and Entrepreneur Evangelist, I search for innovative startups for our venture fund, SV Latam Capital.

I was introduced to StartSe and Felipe five years ago by one of its founders, Marcelo Maisonnave, with whom I had just finished the Executive Program of Singularity University. He knew about my love for Brazilians and how important it is for me to give opportunities for learning not just to people who have come to Silicon Valley with the express purpose to build their startups, but also to people who are still searching for ways to realize their own dreams outside the boundaries of the countries they come from. And that's definitely a big part of StartSe's vision.

So for the last few years, I've been working with StartSe, seeing Felipe in action, and giving pitch workshops to the visiting groups of 100 a wonderful experience full of laughter, learning and joy.

Felipe believes [and this belief is supported by many] that Silicon Valley is one of the main places leading change around the world — showing the best way of managing teams, introducing new business models, and of course, new technologies.

This is a book which aims to teach international professionals how to capture, understand and learn from Felipe's experiences living and working in Silicon Valley. So, if you're an entrepreneur, a businessperson in a small company, or you work in a larger corporation, you'll be able to glean information from the different chapters, understand the SV fundamentals and apply them to your own venture.

— Angelika Blendstrup, Ph.D.
Founding Venture Partner, SV LATAM Fund, Partner @ Startup Embassy, Mentor@500startups & Singularity University

MY STORY

I tell you my story as a means of adding layers of depth and context to the body of work you will soon delve into. And as a way of introducing you to how I arrived at a place where I have developed and am ready to share wisdom with those whose curiosities align with my own.

An immigrant to these United States, I originated from a small town in the countryside of Brazil called Bambuí, where I was born and acquired my first values as person.

While in my early adult years in Brazil, I worked to receive an undergraduate degree in Computing from Pontifical

Catholic University of Minas Gerais and an MBA in Project Management from FGV (Fundação Getulio Vargas).

For fifteen years, I continued to live in Brazil while working in various successful companies and positions there, including playing many key roles at TOTVS, a software company based in São Paulo, Brazil and, according to FGV, leader to the Brazilian ERP market.

Things were going well. I was working in a successful company and growing my career at the same rate as that company. I was granted the opportunity to work on complex projects that challenged me to be a better professional while working with amazing people.

Nothing to complain about, by any means, but something was still missing inside me. The son of enterprising parents, conversations about business were frequent at our dinners, instilling in me from a young age an eternal desire to make a big impact and leave a legacy for the world. And the proper place for this was, as I saw it best, the Silicon Valley.

After finding many successes in a successful career, I decided to challenge myself further, and leave everything I'd ever known behind to move to the Valley, all to study why this place is what it is today: An electrifying ecosystem of innovation.

I was curious to not only understand but to experience firsthand what could make one place so special, as compared with all other places in the world. What could bring such an innovative world to life; one which continues to produce groundbreaking results that level up and affect the rest of the world.

When I first arrived in Silicon Valley, I was invited by Angelika Blendstrup (Ph.D. Stanford and Master's UC Berkeley) — a German friend of mine with over twenty years' experience working in Silicon Valley, and expert in communications and culture exchange — to attend a class held by another friend of hers, Vivek Wadhwa.

Wadhwa teaches classes at Carnegie Mellon University Engineering's Silicon Valley campus located inside NASA's Ames Research Center, where he focuses upon exponential technologies, technology convergence and industry disruption, risks and regulation, and as well the new rules of innovation.

I decided to go with Angelika to witness Wadhwa speak and teach. During this class, Wadhwa at one point said, "An open-minded and diverse population that readily shares information, encourages experimentation, accepts failure and dispenses with formality and hierarchy is what makes Silicon Valley the successful hub that it is."

This hit me like a bullet. A ha! Here is my answer. This man has figured out what makes this place tick! And had worded it so eloquently that I could see clearly, for the first time, some of the reasons for Silicon Valley's consistent growth and development. Now I just needed to experience it firsthand.

So I got to work. And somewhere amidst the many changes I was incorporating, I was invited to attend another event, this time at Greylock partners at the legendary Sand Hill Road (where the world's leading venture capital companies are located), where Reid Hoffman (Founder of LinkedIn) was doing a presentation.

One of the things that struck me most from Hoffman's presentation was where he said, "If you're not embarrassed by the first version of your product, you've launched too late." This led me to instantly leave behind everything I had learned about building successful companies, products and projects, all to rethink the way things are built here in Silicon Valley.

In addition to exploring all that I could of the landscape that is Silicon Valley, I worked to earn a degree in Marketing and Global Business from UC Berkeley, one of the top three universities in the world, and a Master's degree in Computing from International Technological University in San Jose, Silicon Valley.

My various experiences living in this land have led me to delve quite deeply into the reasons that have caused this ecosystem to become such a special place, and I share with you now a collection of the wisdoms I have learned from others, coalesced with much of my own, direct from my thousands of hours of contemplation and exploration into the innovation development scene of The Valley.

Over the past few years, I have begun to take on a key role in the development and creation of StartSe — a startup education platform working to reshape the future of education, focused on training programs geared at the new economy and corporate innovation projects — wherein, I have produced immersion programs to teach executives, entrepreneurs, and investors from around the world the very same teachings presented in this book.

We live in a world that is changing faster and faster, and as a result, people realize that they are becoming professionally obsolete faster and faster as well, and now have a continual and urgent demand to keep up with the innovations and disruptions that appear every day. People have begun to understand and accept the need for A Lifelong Learning Approach, and thus, the need to embark on a path of *continuous reskilling*.

The speed of technological innovations (convergent and exponential) continues to accelerate. These changes drive profound changes in markets, from changes in consumer behavior to the formation of competition; and all this demands new management practices to manage companies, careers and investments. The more management changes, the more energy it returns to evolve technologies and transform markets.

I hold an ecstatic passion for innovation and education, but beyond that, the root of my passion descends from the intense desire to break down innovation in itself, to understand and implement the most useful and essential elements of any conceptual or materialized creation.

Get ready, now, to dive as deeply as I have into the top ten lessons I've learned during my time soaking up The Valley.

CHAPTER ONE

IT ALL STARTS WITH PURPOSE

"If we were motivated by money,
we would have sold the company a long
time ago and ended up on a beach."

— Larry Page, Google

*W**hy* do you do what you do?

Anyone who comes to Silicon Valley arrives here with a purpose. Some idea or ideal driving them to take a risk and invest in themselves.

This investment is so much more than just financial. The investment is a deep, rooted commitment to show up for your goals, and for whatever challenges they bring your way on your pathway to bringing those goals; those dreams to life. The investment is a commitment to stand up for yourself and for what you believe in, no matter the obstacles that cross your path.

This investment is the economy of purpose.

Your purpose is what gives you the motivation to devote yourself to your work. To your business idea, your startup, your venture.

Your purpose is the reason why you take the actions, take the risks, and make the choices you make. It fuels your engine, ignites your passion, and engages the connections with those like-minded individuals who will be with you on the pathway to your success.

So let's establish your purpose. Right here. Right now. Before we begin. Ask yourself now: What is driving you, more than anything, to realize your goals? Why are you doing what you're doing?

And let's go beyond money. Because, of course, we all are in it for the money. But generally, the money is only there to provide for something else. Something that runs much deeper through the wells of your desires.

So why? *Why are you here?*

Knowing your *Why* is what will carry you through the challenges that come across your path. Knowing your *Why* will motivate you on the days you simply can't figure out how to solve the next problem. Be fixed; be *fixated* around what motivates you. And in the tough moments, you can then recall upon your purpose to reignite the passion when things seem exceedingly bleak.

There are always challenges along the path. But most of these challenges don't have to feel so bleak if you can remain flexible with *How* you navigate your *Why*. With a flexibility around how you get to your destination; when you give your journey the freedom to unfold however it needs to unfold, it makes it *that much easier* to get your *Why* to the finish line.

Freeing up your *How* means you don't remain focused on the barriers to entry. You don't focus on the problems; rather, you focus on your purpose. Staying centered around your goals without the judgement of how far or close you seem to realizing them, allows you to free up your focus for staying committed to taking the small action steps that dissolve any limitations or challenges you face.

A grounded mission will perpetuate your business past simple profits.

Your mission is the *heart* of your startup, company, venture. It serves as the foundation for a transformational business venture to be built upon. And while this may seem *basic*, to speak so invasively to the obvious idea of "purpose", I harp only because I see how considerably the strength of purpose can make or break a business.

Especially in the current times of mission-based conscious consumerism, social causes now absolutely *must* be embedded into the very fiber of the business model. The veil has become too thin, and accountability is on an ever-increasing rise. The fat must be trimmed eventually, and in the societal current, startups, companies, and ventures of all kinds can be slashed and crumble straight to the ground without this firm foundation of purpose supporting them.

Purpose goes beyond a simple idea. Purpose is taking action on your beliefs.

You have to *be it* to believe it. And *believe* it or not, it's not the other way around. Be the purpose; become one with the heart of your business, and you will walk the venture path with So Much More conviction, reassurance and honestly... luck!

When your business is led by a meaningful purpose (not just one that sounds good, but one that truly means something to you; truly makes you feel something), the right people and timing show up as if by magic. Thing is, there's no magic to it! There's neuroscience, there's biology, there's marketing... and it all points to the truth that our motivations drive us to take action.

When you want an investor, a customer, a team member to take action with your business, you need to motivate them. You do this by making them truly *feel* something for your work.

None of this purpose talk is fluff. I'm not writing this to say things that sound good. Truly, completely, honestly, a heart-led purpose makes *all* the difference in your venture. When you put your purpose before your profits, and you make it the cornerstone of your business, your decisions naturally align with this purpose, igniting and encouraging authenticity in your pursuit.

In other words, when you are able to communicate clearly your *Why*, your value proposition will organically differentiate your brand from all the "me too" products in the world.

Look at some of the standalone brands of our age. Asana, Airbnb, Uber... each of these is centered around a deeply anchored mission. Asana's mission statement states: "To help humanity thrive by enabling all teams to work together effortlessly."

Would you think that, when you think of Asana? Not necessarily. Your needs are met, your workload gets easier, and you move on to the next tool. But still, the relief you feel from the success of this tool was motivated by this mission, of helping humanity to *thrive* through effortless co-creation.

Uber's mission statement is, "Transportation as reliable as running water, everywhere for everyone." *Muah! Incredible!* If I didn't know what company's mission I was reading, I would still hop on board instantly. Meaningful work – poetic, even! And for a final killer example of a mission, I bring to your attention Airbnb with their: "To connect millions of people in real life all over the world, through a community marketplace – so that you can Belong Anywhere."

Your purpose can create just as much of a cultural impact as it does a financial one, and generally the two go hand in hand. This alone showcases just how serious this purpose business is. The Burson-Marsteller/IMD Power of Purpose Study states how "an authentic and well-communicated purpose can contribute to the results and success of a mission." [1]

Discovering your *Why* naturally allows you to make better decisions. Decisions borne out of clarity, rather than confusion. Those who know their *Why* naturally find more of the success so many of us angstily search for.

Stop the angst. **Start** the commitment to yourself. Investing in the difficult moments, and showing up for your *Why*, even when all else may seem lost.

Remember those questions you asked yourself earlier? Take another look at your *Why*. Now, ask yourself if your *Why* is strong enough to carry you through all the doubt, the worry, the fear, the confusion. Ask yourself if your why will be there like a beacon of hope shining through.

And if you think that it is; that it will be there for you, then you are ready to begin.

Innovation grows from passionate purpose. Purpose is a sustainable business model. A sustainable environment to grow your seedling into a successful creation.

When your purpose is rooted in how you show up for your business, others will naturally be inspired by it. Inspired to show up for you, excited to be on your team, and moved to be a part of your greater venture vision.

Sure! You can totally just have a great idea, put the work in, and meet all your goals. Totally. But *something* will have to give eventually, and if you're without a purpose, your chances of getting sidetracked, or making choices that don't bring you to your goal, are all that much higher. Your purpose drives your decisions in the direction of your vision.

From this place, like a horse right out the gate, you are bound for the completion of your goals; and what's even better, your purpose will keep you pointed in the right direction. Your true north.

What's your true north? Your cause? Your belief? *Why* even do what you're wanting to do?

I don't ask this to challenge you. I ask this to support you in having what you need to breed the success you desire.

Dig into any discomfort that may rise up as confusion. Like an archaeologist, comb through the dust and dirt until you reveal the treasure trove of Who You Are and what authentically motivates you.

No one wants your great idea, so much as they want your great idea to make them feel good. Happy, inspired, free to be themselves. Wherever their motivation drives them, is *through* feeling. Your buyers, your teammates, your collaborators want to feel understood, want to trust you, want to feel happy and motivated... and you get all this through sharing your passion; your *Why*, with those you work with, in whatever capacity!

Just as a teammate will give you everything they have, work overtime, and without complaint when they believe in the mission and purpose of the work they are doing, as too will an investor, a partner, a team member, a collaborator be more invested in their work when they feel your passion, your purpose; when they align with it and love the pursuit with a passion.

"62% of people say they prefer to work for a company that gives back to society and makes them feel like they are working to make a positive difference in the world. That is why purpose-driven startups attract smart and passionate people." [2]

Success is better collective, than alone.

Authority is something you command; leadership is what you present.

Use your purpose to lead others who feel as you do. Without the need to command authority, force or push connections, or make anyone uncomfortable "for the good of the company". Use your *Why* to build your team, and to motivate the investors who think like you do; who feel how you feel, to journey with you on your venture.

Use your purpose to guide how you communicate how you are unique in your venture. To your investors, to your teammates, to your consumers.

Others will invest in you when you invest in yourself. So dig in as deep as is necessary. Fight the internal battles and turmoil of any doubt, confusion or fears. And in turn, draw out your passion like a poison whip that will charge through the limitations and barriers. That may even dissolve them, leaving your path that much clearer for the correct kind of focus to drive forth your vision.

Whenever business is led by a heart-based mission, consumers are more able to connect to and engage with the business' core idea, creating meaningful impact at each and every touchpoint. When your mission is clear, you naturally invite others into your story, empowering them to take up arms and stand next to you; with you, in communicating your purpose to the wider whole. You bring people together, allowing them to feel valued and valuable in how they direct their dollar.

Then, they are no longer a simple consumer, but a lifelong supporter and loyal customer.

Wielding your purpose — your *Why* — with clarity leads to a fulfilling business value, as well as an organically higher profitability. Proving, once and for all, just how essential an element purpose is in the aim for any venture success.

CHAPTER TWO

BUILD A GREAT TEAM, IT WILL BUILD A GREAT PRODUCT

"The secret to successful hiring is this: look for the people who want to change the world."

— Marc Benioff, Salesforce

How do you turn your purpose into a product?

Hard work? Yes, of course.

Skill sets? Yes, definitely.

But, even possessing these things, can *you alone* bring a successful product to market before your idea is no longer applicable (especially in the time of tech)?

No, most assuredly, you cannot.

All good things take time. But how do you use that time wisely?

You assemble a team. A team of mighty giants ready to topple themselves over to rebuild the world in a collective vision.

This sounds so great! Yes, but this can be the most difficult thing in the entire process to create.

It takes a raw honesty and a fearless ability to lead through integrity, bravery and grace. It takes a personal investment to choose not to entertain the old ways of viewing "employees" as worker bees; but rather, to choose to search for those who are more advanced than you and can contribute as an equal to the collective vision which you lead.

Your team is far more important than most business owners, developers or executives generally consider. That old era of workhorses is over, and where it isn't over, businesses are hemorrhaging — many, thanks to the Silicon Valley innovators of teamwork research and development.

In the same way you approach your purpose in your venture, your best approach with your team is to search intuitively and cognitively for those who are healthily passionate; who hold their heart hand in hand with their business acumen.

Taking more time, and focusing more attention on the *Who* of your company can be an incredible approach to front-loading your venture's success.

Founder of the prestigious Y Combinator accelerator, Sam Altman, has said, "Mediocre people at a big company cause some problems, but they don't usually kill the company. A single mediocre hire in the first five will kill a startup."

It is vitally ever that much more important, when you are building a startup, to take ample time building your team, while always remaining willing to release those whose values show themselves not to align with those of your greater business vision, mission and values; as well as your own personal values, if you are the cornerstone of your company (as most of you reading this book most likely are).

So many startups fail; so many businesses crumble, all because of poor team management. If you're in Silicon Valley, or somehow else engaged as an innovator of the western world, you'll need to be critically engaged with the process of building or developing your team.

You assess your potential team members by aligning where their values, vision and mission align with yours. These aspects of your business are the bedrock of your collective success. Together, you can go so much farther than alone.

So long as your venture is in the process of growing, you are in the mindspace of hiring, and each new member contributes to the greater whole. Only, instead of the previously conceived notion of the more members, the less each individual matter; the truth of the matter is that the more members you have, the potential less awareness you are able to have over how your team is working overall towards the venture's greater goals.

The more you rely on communication to occur between individuals you've never met or may not have time to connect with on a regular basis, the less viable trust you build within your business. The less likely the chance for success.

It has been proven that the more personally invested a teammate is in the brand they represent, the better their work. And though this is a practice long held, relying on a team you don't personally know can cause massive sinkholes in productivity if the wrong members are welcomed aboard.

Like a domino effect, the wrong twist or turn, and the whole of the work can collapse... while you watch from your ivory tower, thinking maybe it was someone else's fault for the destruction.

The current times would argue that it was, instead, directly the fault of the one key individual holding the team up. The leader.

Your team brings your vision; your product to life, remember. Your vision has to be the leader to point your teammates' vision in the right direction.

When each and every team member has been cherry-picked and has proven their trustworthiness through time and committed attention while given support for their individual growth amidst the team, the team members are more apt to root for the success of their team. This way, the more likely they are to pursue their goals with a passion, giving their best!

Then, with the company's vision and values at the forefront of their minds and personal interests (instead of at the back of their thoughts, regretting having to go to work) they can then bring in other potential team members with that same quality. Like attracts like, and with it, weaves a web of massive connectivity coiled around one core principle: TRUST.

Team dynamics are an essential aspect to the success of your venture.

Choose those who are aligned with your business goals. Find as much cohesion as you can with those you bring into your circle, rather than making the mistake so many founders do, of choosing a random selection of contacts and quick finds for their startup team.

Even if you are a CEO or executive to a developed corporation, team hires are becoming more and more recognized as the heartbeat of the business. Large teams are taking longer than ever before to hire, executives taking a much more hands on approach to hiring from within or with direct internal reference, rather than hiring outsiders.

You see, trust is generally a key value of any employer-hiree relationship, and it holds quite a high value, indeed.

Trust: That elusive cohabitative idea we each try to suss out from others. No matter the relationship, we strive to trust others. We do our best to trust ourselves, and unfortunately, we often have to work the hardest to trust those we work with.

Business and trust don't go hand in hand often enough. And a history of bad blood between the two has strewn trust's reputation across time as nonexistent in business.

This is changing. Though there's a long trek uphill still to take, many executives are coming to terms with the truth of the importance of trust in teamwork.

I was at John Couch's house for dinner on the 4th of July this year. Former Apple VP of education, Couch was *personally hired* by Steve Jobs. At dinner, he said something that struck me, when I asked what he did to motivate himself to keep learning. He replied, "I've always hired better people than me, so I could learn from them."

Many key innovators of our era are known for choosing to devote more of their time to building and knowing their team members on a much more personal level than has been practiced in the past.

Dave Gilboa, Warby Parker cofounder, spends over 25% of his time on recruitment alone! What's even more, Mark Zuckerberg, CEO of Facebook, is known to spend nearly half of his time in recruiting talent alone — something he apparently adopted from legend Steve Jobs.

Zuckerberg would often go on long walks with his potential hires, to ensure he got to know each individual's authentic nature by the time they parted ways.

Another rock-solid example here comes from the so-called "PayPal Mafia". Paypal was built up of a team of innovation giants, each one finding post-PayPal success of the highest degree. So many of the former founders found true tech success after PayPal, and they all attributed that success to something they learned from their time spent working on the PayPal team: Having a successful startup team is the framework for modeling all innovation from there on out.

This is why interviewing each potential hire has got to be an authentic engagement. Has absolutely got to be a true conversation, rather than the traditional question-and-answer session of listing off an itemized list of experiences, values and qualities.

You'll get a resume. So don't spend the interview time beating a dead horse. Inquire more deeply into the individual's values, traditions, passions, virtues, and favorite successes and failures. Ask them about their favorite work environments, and what led them to search for a new opportunity. Have an exit interview, only upon entrance, to see how their ideas will truly contribute to the culture and innovation of your team as a whole.

Successful metrics and track records are great, of course they are, but they will not allow you to see whether your potential new hire will be a positive attribution to the team as a whole. Often, the reverse is actually true! Amazing team members may have an odd and unusual history, so don't let that turn you away from really connecting, listening to and observing each individual you assess.

Be sure to fully show up for your team members, the way you want them to show up for you, as a means of leading by example in your endeavors.

When building the team that will build your product, the most important aspect to gauge is the attitude. Would you want to spend a lot of time with them, outside of their skill sets and value?

If yes, this may be an intuitive hit that they are perfect for your team. Dig into that, as it is often a sign that you've found someone who is deeply aligned with the core values of your venture.

Ask what the person did in practice. Ask them about their values and how they ENACT them in their daily lives. And of course presenting hypothetical problems for them to communicate to you how they would solve can support you in sussing out the right person for the right job.

Lastly, don't just consider what they can do for you, but what you can do for them as well. If they have something to learn or gain that aligns with their overarching life goals, all the better, as sussing this out will help you to see why and how they will be motivated to work under your leadership.

Slack, a wildly popular team management system, is quoted as "the fastest-growing business application in history." But what's even more impressive about them is how they've set themselves apart in their interpersonal relations.

Slack's cofounder, Stewart Butterfield, has shared how a large part of their success is attributed to how they worked as a team to set themselves apart from any other company out there. They used their own team as an example for how to create their successful product.

They created a whole team just to support and solve customer queries, actively listening to all the feedback they could absorb. And their strategy?

To invite clients to their team meetings, just to show them how to use the platform effectively for their unique needs. The customer was not only king, but queen and country as well! By providing their customers with these one-on-one, crafted sessions, clients were able to feel how working with the product would be moving forward. They were encouraged to try the product, risk free, and when they had opinions, the Slack team was there to incorporate them with care!

Use this same approach when building your team. Engage them with your product so they can begin to feel a personal investment with what they will work alongside you to grow. Allowing this freedom for personalized self-expression in the workplace will be the biggest (albeit cheapest) investment you could make!

CHAPTER THREE

CULTURE EATS STRATEGY FOR BREAKFAST

"Why is culture so important to a business? Here is a simple way to frame it. The stronger the culture, the less corporate process a company needs. When the culture is strong, you can trust everyone to do the right thing."

— Brian Chesky, Airbnb

Writer, teacher and business visionary Simon Sinek once pointed out how, "Corporate culture matters. How management chooses to treat its people impacts everything for better or for worse."

Along with the idea of building a team with aligned values, vision and mission, the culture developed within and for the team will carry it through the long Mondays and sudden changes.

We'll all be honest here, and admit that no matter how passionate we are, we will feel, at times, a variant in our work. Something which interjects itself into our lives and disrupts our flow. Perhaps it's just a bad day, perhaps something spinning chaos through each fiber of our lives.

No matter what, it makes all the difference when you feel you can be yourself and feel supported in your work environment.

Consider this when building and developing the culture of your company.

From retaining quality talent to boosting your profile with investors, quality culture will transform a workplace from a lifeless machine to a self-evolving AI of innovation, continuously exciting all those who engage with it.

Creating a powerful culture starts with the people involved in it. Thus, it absolutely must be developed from a place of authenticity. From a space of digging in to reveal the truth of what will most genuinely engage teammates and encourage them to get personally involved in cultivating it.

Authentic culture cannot be developed through any semblance of strategy. It becomes null and void in the face of real human interface.

Save the strategy for the product or service your business will provide, and do not fear becoming entwined within the culture of your workplace. Should you show up fully to engage with your team members, the impact your presence makes will not go unnoticed.

Lead by example. Showcase the ideals of your company culture in how you engage in the society it has created. In the ecosystem which lives there! This inspires your team members to see firsthand the impact of embodying the values and vision of the company they work for; the team they work with.

And through your embodiment, ensure your team members feel free to speak their minds. If you must, find a way to learn how to be a quality listener. Rather than rely on HR, inspire your HR team members to engage with others on the team through how you engage with *them*.

Strategy is perfect for guiding decision making and igniting forward momentum, but expending the efforts to create a quality culture for your team to fall back on cannot be overlooked. So many of us have had poor experiences in toxic workplaces that cultural overhaul is one of the frontiers of the Silicon Valley way.

I've learned, through my experiences working with startups and ventures of all kinds, that culture comes first.

So, here we are. Step one: Find your purpose. Step two: Build a quality team who aligns with that purpose. Step three: Build a culture that team can rely on and become part of on a deeper level to drive innovation in their every interaction with their work.

The hope is for your team to uncover together a flow that allows them to feel they are living their best life while working to make your vision a reality. This breeds quality habits that infuse themselves into all workplace activities. As I've said before, the endeavor is an ecosystem you build from the ground up. Each element you incorporate is essential to how that ecosystem lives and breathes on its own.

And culture is the harbinger of this ecosystem.

Culture involves all personnel-related aspects of the workspace. From how you handle vacation policies to allowing a level of flexible workflow, your choices in this area should not be doled out to HR to decide. These aspects directly affect your team members, so choosing wisely and with a nurturing approach can make a large impact on your overall productivity and evolution.

Culture, quite honestly, holds your company together. A company's culture is largely an output of the people who work there. With or without you present, it continues to grow on its own accord. A fantastic work culture can even help to sell the image of the company.

Culture is set by the leaders, starting with the founders.

Culture is set early and is hard to change.

Let's move together through some beloved workplaces as a point of example for how to build and nurture your own company culture.

Twitter, for example, is one of those companies whose workers can't stop raving about them. Team members love their lives, and love the culture their workplace provides.

They often hold their meetings on their building's rooftop, including free food, which is also offered at their San Francisco headquarters on a regular basis. From yoga classes to unlimited vacation time for higher ups, their team is an assembly of friendly, team-oriented individuals who each feel uniquely motivated to work passionately towards the company's greater goals.

They are certainly doing something right. And that something has a lot to do with showing appreciation through cultural development. Showing encouragement and showering praise through acts of nourishment.

Google is one of those companies with one of the best reputations for culture out there. If anything, Google has set the tone for what is now almost expected for a company to provide when it comes to cultural support.

They offer team members trips, parties, continuous free food, open learning opportunities with high-level executives, a plethora of opportunities for physical engagement throughout the workday and even a dog-friendly workspace. As a result, Googlers are renowned for their talent, drive, and for setting themselves apart from the herd.

Certainly an interesting company to watch when it comes to culture, Google has been challenged to keep their cultural pace as they've expanded over the years. Between headquarters and satellite offices, the larger their — or any — company becomes, the more the culture has to evolve to continue to support the team through its many changes.

Google is a very competitive workplace, as so many Silicon Valley outfits are. I see their biggest challenge as one where they have to be able to nurture their teammates in a way that doesn't douse their drive as it works to encourage healthy habits.

Even the most resolute of workplaces needs to revisit its culture as it grows and changes, so as to ensure it evolves with the times. Every successful business is built upon a successful culture.

Besides the usual amenities, Facebook focuses their culture around the ideals of teamwork, open communication and an atmosphere that fosters and nurtures personal development. As well, Facebook has managed to explode in growth while continuing to remain synonymous with a unique company culture.

Yet, Facebook still struggles with what so many titan companies do: Highly competitive industry standards that lead to an undeniably competitive workplace.

To solve this problem, Facebook innovated outdoor roaming spaces for use by all teammates, as well as open office space where executives work alongside other teammates. All as a pursuit toward creating an open culture where the space itself promotes a sense of self-motivated action steps and equality amongst teammates.

When you're running a company highly dependent on cultivating new hires with a record of excellence in a highly competitive field like Facebook, the culture and perks you offer your team will often be the tipping point, so no matter the resources you have available to you, doing what you can to creatively supply a nurturing space can make or break the caliber of teammates you're able to bring on board.

And remember to **be intentional** about your culture to keep it sustainable, to ensure it won't combust or shatter, having been hanging by a thread for too long.

Choose wisely how you support your workplace culture. Wouldn't it be great for your team to consider your company as their number one place to work? I see it as the most useful marketing tactic to date, and one many Silicon Valley companies strive to provide as a marker of success along the pathway to a peaceful exit, or whatever their goals might be.

So many of the companies out here, however, get stuck shouting in the Silicon Valley echo chamber, where they obsess over who's working with who, who's made the most contacts, raised the most money, has the most stock... a competitive yet hollow place to remain. One without much room for growth or innovation, as competitive mindsets don't nurture innovation and creative expression the way a healthy and free workspace does.

If you're part of a well-established, larger company, your challenge may be in shifting an entrenched and potentially hazardous culture. Established cultures are more difficult to change, to be sure, but it can be done. Maybe the culture worked for the company when they were first developing, but was left behind long ago and stopped evolving as the company did.

If you are looking to solve issues in your workplace morale, look to the culture. Do as Facebook did, and get creative with how you can culturally shift into something healthier and more cooperative for all. Dig into how your values can be reignited through the ways in which you breathe a new cultural atmosphere into your workplace, to set the tone for where you would like to see a shift occur in the future.

And whether or not you have the budget to pay your teammates their dream salary and offer unlimited vacation time, you can still build the same quality culture by choosing how you support it in more creative ways which encourage your people to truly buy into the company mission.

Developing a company culture full of heart and empowerment is a fantastic and economical way to motivate your teammates when aspects of the compensation package aren't as stable as other competitors.

Workers rave when they feel like they are an essential part of a company that is doing something to make a positive impact in the world. There is often a sense in these workspaces that no one wants to leave until the work is complete. This energy is *priceless*.

You can't beat having team members who are pleasant and friendly to each other, and are both good at and love what they are doing. No program, activity or set of rules tops having happy and fulfilled teammates who feel that what they are doing matters.

CHAPTER FOUR

OWNERSHIP MENTALITY

"It doesn't make sense to hire smart people and tell them what to do; we hire smart people so they can tell us what to do."

— Steve Jobs, Apple

I am a firm believer in owning the experiences of your life, rather than playing the victim to what happens in your life. Life, after all, is not happening to you... it's happening through you. You play a vital role in the life you lead, based on how you choose to react rather than respond to your surroundings.

Many individuals will not understand the importance of maintaining this sense of integrity in life, let alone bring this mentality into business.

So how can you encourage this in the workspace?

Some useful ways, we have already discussed. The company culture, for one. Use this as a means of bringing to life the ownership you hope for your teammates to have over their work.

Another way to encourage integrity and ownership mentality is to allow your teammates a sense of freedom in the workplace, so they feel empowered in their tasks, no matter what they might be doing.

You can also ensure an ownership mentality through the hiring process, by communicating openly and transparently around expectations and desires. As an aside, a sense of transparency in itself nurtures ownership culture to grow.

Enable your teammates to build true ownership in the business by encouraging them to think and act like businesspeople in their own right, rather than hired hands.

Inspire them by giving them the freedom to play their way through their workday, moving at their own pace to achieve their goals. In this way, you sit back as the leader, guiding them down the pathway, rather than forcing them blind into the darkness and confusion of micromanagement and workhorse mentality.

In this way, they are self-guided and self-motivated. The work they do for your business is *their* work for *their* business.

This idea of teammate ownership has been the lifeblood of Silicon Valley thinking for over 30 years. And that same old story of the part-timer who hit it big has drawn thousands more talented teammates into the startup ecosystem since that time.

Teammates from successful startups in the Valley often go on to start their own companies, or to invest in the next generation of startups as angels. Thus, a cycle of entrepreneurship is fostered. A cycle based upon the ideal of ownership as the key factor of integral business practice.

The people who make up your organization are the most valuable part of that organization, and the value that supports this cycle. The most coveted teammates of any industry are the ones who own their work by going above and beyond.

And when you ask them why... it's because they feel empowered to do their best work. They take pride in their work. They feel personally driven to do what they can for the company's highest good.

Owners feel they have something to gain, or something to lose, based off of their individual level of performance. And what's more, is they believe in the work they do, and believe they are making a positive impact on the world, albeit in some small way, by being a part of your greater mission.

Owners can only be owners when they feel like they won't be blamed or bullied into working. Their efforts come from a motivation within; a personal motivation to do their best.

Regrettably, according to Gallup's State of the American Workplace report, only an approximate one-third of employees feel like owners.[1]

And a whole 'nother 50 percent play the role of "job renters," working as though they are drones on an assembly line in need of more oil. They come to work, but they never truly *show up*, bringing their full selves to the table. They keep a low profile.

The rest of the teammates you'll see as the outliers. Actively disengaged, perhaps even purposely sabotaging workplace momentum, whether consciously or subconsciously.

A teammate will go far beyond merely taking responsibility when they feel a sense of ownership over their work. When they feel a personal investment in what they do. This is where innovation becomes a part of the mix. When the mind is in a personally engaged level of attention, more creative activations can occur, thus breeding broader and more expansive ideas that are then brought to the table to be observed and processed by the entire team.

Leadership determines the potential space for individual motivation. So many workers are easily and directly affected by the ecosystem they work within, so it is imperative for team leaders to encourage this freedom and activate this trust.

As well, it is important to clearly establish the unique assets to working on your team through clear goal setting and showcasing brand development. This sparks within your team members a deep desire to support something special, compounding the potential for them to develop their own sense of ownership.

To grow your company as quickly as you need to these days, you will want to take advantage of every opportunity to build trust with your teammates. Encourage this trust by being transparent with business happenings, keeping doors open during meetings, or even taking a meeting outdoors to loosen up the tone if needed.

One way I see nearly all Silicon Valley companies quickly build and instill this trust is by offering stock options to their teammates. The way the Valley sees it, you absolutely must have a meritocracy-based system implemented early on, as people who think and act as owners must actually own the business, as well, to fully integrate into your vision.

No one wants to build or enrich other people as much as they do themselves, at the end of the day. A partnership model will ensure the owner mentality in practice. If they think and act as owners, they must be owners, as well. And if the company succeeds, they, too, soon need to be part of this success.

Be as much of an owner in how you approach your team as you would like for them to be with their work. Always be the example through how you lead.

In this vein, be sure to implement practices which not only allow your teammates to feel free to follow their own workflow, but free to speak their minds and share their opinions, as well. Increase ownership by ensuring your workers feel valued and listened to.

When you can even, then, allow everyone on your team to feel free to take self-engineered, calculated risks, ownership will blossom before you, because the individuals will feel more limitless in asserting their own creative vision.

It is important to mention about creating an environment where teammates can realize their dreams within the company. Entrepreneurial people want to work in their own company, in their own projects. Create an environment where you can maximize the potential of entrepreneurs within your company.

Steve Jobs was a master of creating a space where team members felt free to own their work, allowing them the space to do small things; like, for example, add developer names to the plastic cover of the Macintosh.

Only in Silicon Valley do I see leaders who truly take the time to listen to those under their watch, and then apply or work to implement new ideas that come from the bottom up. The right leader can alone inspire ownership in the workplace, and it can be done through simple means of ensuring all team members feel valued.

Quality leaders understand the vital importance of aligned goals. They value the personal goals of their teammates as they know shared goals are the most innovative way of encouraging ownership.

Quality leaders understand that they do not own their teammates. Their teammates then feel the freedom to take their own power back from the old workhorse paradigms, and empower themselves to become owners of their own careers, and the work they do each day.

CHAPTER FIVE

THINK DIFFERENT

"A diverse mix of voices leads to better discussions, decisions, and outcomes for everyone."

— Sundar Pichai, Google

Diversity is one of Silicon Valley's most secret sauces.

Diversity is the root of invention.

When you're in the process of hiring, be sure to avoid bringing in people with too many similar traits and backgrounds. Instead, look for some outliers and surprises. Allow yourself to be surprised with who you hire, and look instead for aligned principles. A diversity amongst team members' personalities and experiences will bring the potential for more fresh ideas and unique, complementary collaborative traits.

When you still search for shared value systems, throughout all the diversity you bring in, you are ensuring your teammates' values align with your business' core values while still allowing freedom for limitless expansion.

Airbnb was not created by a group of hotel experts; rather, it was created by a group of guys who got their feet wet in the world of innovation by creating a limited-edition series of cereal boxes. Similar stories hold true for the creators of Uber, WhatsApp, and so many more.

Diversity breeds innovation.

If these companies had consulted best practices within the industry of their product, the solutions they found would have been determined by the knowledge base of how things are already done in that field.

Some of the most ignorant of ideas from the most unlikely of sources can end up producing the most innovative solutions to industry problems. So get creative with your team, and as well with the diversity of how your team incorporates and collaborates, to encourage a diverse approach to problem solving.

Differences in business visions, perspectives and ways of thinking make up the diversity that disrupts Silicon Valley in creative and innovative ways!

For example, Amazon pledged, in 2016, to hire 25,000 veterans and military spouses within five years of their initial pledge, while training 10,000 separate veterans in cloud computing.

This was no small feat, and it made just as large of an impact on the Amazon brand. Yet, even fairly small efforts can have a wonderful compounding effect when carried out with authentic passion. By creating and nurturing authenticity in the very spaces you're supporting with your business, you market yourself as relevant; only, your marketing budget is going towards a genuine humanitarian effort rather than advertising, of which there is already plenty!

From experience and expertise to problem solving, skills and approaches, cultural differences offer unique perspectives which combine and culminate in fascinating ways to add to the collective goal being seen and built from that many more angles.

Silicon Valley is your quintessential melting pot, as those who live and work here come from all across the globe, bringing more than 100 differing dialects with them. Diverse thinking comes easily here, and in California people are generally more willing to be openly themselves in the workplace.

In some regions of the world, this is not the case, and you may need to pull the personality out of someone through showcasing to them the trust that they are indeed free to do so!

Where diversity is encouraged by company founders, productivity, creativity and innovation soar! A more entrepreneurial mindset is provoked, leading to a keen sensibility for creative problem solving, adaptability and responsiveness to market changes and trends.

Ensure you encourage and cultivate a plethora of diversity in your company to surround yourself with a unique and innovative think tank!

Best-selling author Adam Grant often said, instead of looking for those who will be a potentially good "cultural fit" for your workplace, look for those who would make a cultural *contribution* to the team overall. [1]

Innovative thinkers are unique by nature. So be open to not judge anyone's book by their cover, and attempt to remain open to what they bring to the table. Not many people respond well to a fresh, innovative and never-before-seen idea the first time out of the gate.

So be unique in this way, as well. Take the ideas and opinions and handle them all with care. Engage fully with as open a mind and as little judgement as you can to:
1. Ensure you are building trust within your team, and
2. Cultivate limitless growth and expansion potential for your product or venture.

Originality cannot be overlooked. In advance to seeking out diversity, assess where your company culture is lacking or has bottomed out, and bring in someone with the energy to change things up and enliven the dynamics at play.

When you take this approach, you not only foster the diversity to grow beyond traditional constructs, such as age, gender, ethnicity, interests and religion, but as well, diverse perspectives begin to evolve from the unique combinations abounding, thus creating the bold, big ideas every venture years for.

Generally, you can find two different types of people in organizations. One type are the givers, excitable and willing to contribute to whatever is at play; and the other are the takers, mostly looking out for themselves in the workplace and in life. Takers are generally not team players, so when interviewing, be sure to assess whether this "winner takes all" mindset underlies any potential new hires.

I bring this up because takers can damage your bottom line, and without realizing it, breed toxicity in the workplace. Like a sickness, the "me first" mindset sucks the creativity and zaps the innovation out of a place in a flash. Thus, distinguishing between the two is of vital importance, not only for your bottom line, but as well for what it can cost your culture.

Often, we believe kindness communicates a giving sensibility, but this is not always the case. Often, resentment lives under the surface, in the subconscious, and can sneak up when things start to turn for the worst.

"Giving and taking are your deep-down motives," Adam Grant has said on the matter, "whereas [whether you are] agreeable or disagreeable is just your surface veneer."[2]

This an essential point to understand, as the golden combination comes when you can find someone who qualifies as a "disagreeable giver". One who is skeptical yet committed to the team goals will be your greatest asset as an agent for change.

Though difficult to spot, learning to recognize these kinds of differing personality traits will support your team diversity. Finding individuals who move against the collective current, yet remain committed to the overall goal, will use their coarseness to add a nice, smooth finish to your project.

No matter where your search for diversity leads you, and no matter how and where it engages with your business, remember to keep your mind open to entertain new perspectives while searching for those deeply rooted, internal value systems that align with and support your own.

In other words, hire for aligned vision, values and missions, not aligned experience or background. Look for diversity there to breed your innovation without compromising your overall goals.

CHAPTER SIX

FOCUS ON EXECUTION AND INTENSITY

"I think the high-tech industry is used to developing new things very quickly. It's the Silicon Valley way of doing business: You either move very quickly and you work hard to improve your product technology, or you get destroyed by some other company."

— Elon Musk

Another key element to implement into your teamwork dreamwork is a laser focus on execution and intensity in all that you build. This means letting ideas be ideas, but when it comes to taking action, doing so with a sense of absolute accuracy and precision. Foregoing hesitation while aiming acutely at the opportunities that lie before you.

Startup guru Steve Blank's mantra is to "get out of the building" to test and validate your product as soon as you can, and often. The entrepreneurs of the Valley aren't afraid to get their hands dirty, go out to the sidewalks, and engage with their personas. You can think and plan and study and track all that you want, for as long as you want. But contact, touchpoints, real live data and research speak bounds in comparison.

Months in the studio developing an idea can result in poor user experience that trumps all the time spent adjusting. Don't be afraid to engage your business, in whatever way it delivers product to consumer, and sooner rather than later.

Ideas are transient, slippery, elusive things. They can make or break success, sure, but they are always there. Without a developed product to share with your users, however, your ideas will not bring in any business.

The great entrepreneurs are focused on implementing their idea while the idealists are still perfecting the thought. Be great in how you approach your project development, and do so with execution and intensity to move the actionable steps forward. Do so with fire and brimstone at your heels, if you must!

Google was not the first search engine to be thought up, but it is by far the most successful in its field to date. The same goes for Facebook as a social network, Groupon, Spotify and so many others. What they did successfully was integrate and develop a product ten times better than anything else out there by tweaking and improving their user experience!

How do you think they did that?

Well, they got down to business... executing their ideas through facilitating an intense and interpersonal engagement between the user and the product the team was working to improve.

What's more is that all the while, they were also working to build and sustain a successful business to support their product as it became successful in itself.

Oh, the many moving parts to the process…. The only way to make it through is, really, to remain focused, all eyes forward on bringing the vision to life, doing everything necessary to adjust the product along the way.

It is one beautiful thing, alright, to witness an entrepreneur obsessed. However, there is something much more powerful about an entrepreneur who is able to move out of the obsession of the idea or the sheer innovation, and able to move into a state of obsession with the actual execution of that idea.

Don't let your team get stuck in ideation phase one. Don't get stuck there, yourself! Keep the momentum moving through the execution stage, through engaging the product with the user, and through bringing it to market.

Perfectionists aren't pretty, and they don't make pretty things. Stay grounded and take one step after the other so as to maintain a healthy relationship, and encourage a healthy relationship with the product, startup, or venture that has your heart in its grasp.

You may be surprised at how many just okay ideas have turned out to be really well-executed products. So don't get caught up in ideas, perfection, or doubt. And do try to trust the timing of your growth.

Trust me, from all I have learned in my time here, it's when you're worried you're too late that you most likely have the timing just right. So if you're sitting there terrified you've missed your window of opportunity, it may just mean you're finally ready and so is the world ready to receive what you have to offer!

Stay present and stay focused. And trust in the process!

Just because an idea fails doesn't mean it's wrong. Heck most products fail. Most businesses fail. But, it's in the failures that the successes are found, cultivated and developed.

Nailing the timing of a release can prove to be the most difficult aspect of innovation, often leaving hundreds of products in recycling bins, either because they were too late or because they were too early. However, the innovation continues. These early adaptations set the groundwork for the future ones to come.

Often times the idealists are the ones who come a bit too early to the table, while the pragmatists show up on time or even a little late to the party, but with a plan ready to be promoted and a product ready to be implemented.

One more reason to get your product out there, and execute. While an idea isn't the end all of a business, what matters most is the execution and timing.

When the market exists, and the timing is aligned, really all you need to do to make your business a success is to apply it. If it succeeds, if it fails, it is no matter... it is a success either way because of the process you applied to it.

In any business, operational excellence must coalesce smoothly with the people carrying it out. A business will depend on its ability to smoothly merge with technological elements in order to optimize its return, as well as maintain a competitive positioning.

More often than we'd like to be true, any entrepreneur will create a remarkable new product or platform without considering some of the most basic adaptations and evolutions which must occur to bring the new idea its success. The tech, the processes, the people, and most importantly the business model must be in an intrepid process of evolution.

All elements of the business must continuously evolve and improve as the product or platform does. If this evolution is not universal throughout the business, it will crumble or, worse, never reach its potential.

Ask yourself if your attention is focused across the board, or if you, like so many before you, are justifying dropping the ball in some areas in exchange for all focus directed at the product /platform.

And be sure to adjust! Your business and you are cohesively organic. Be prepared for your own evolution, and be resilient as you are called upon to change every element in support of the greater growth.

What matters is the ability and drive to execute. The ability to engage change in your next steps, with precision and focus on moving forward.

Stay focused, and be sure to execute your ideations... the sooner the better!

CHAPTER SEVEN

FAIL FAST

"I've probably failed more often than anybody else in Silicon Valley. Those don't matter. I don't remember the failures. You remember the big successes."

— Vinod Khosla, Sun Microsystems

Me? Failure? Oh, yes. A big hell yes here.

No one wants to fail. But I've failed a lot. But you know what? I've failed about as often and as much as any other innovator, and now I have more badges of honor to showcase all the rich, lush, variant experiences my failures have brought my way as useful data to incorporate into any and all future ventures.

When building something new, or bringing to light something raw and fresh, the potential for failure is higher, because chances are, the market isn't ready, even when the product is great.

But all along the way there, all throughout the process, are a million little failures, scattered like breadcrumbs leading the way to the ultimate success.

If you can remain focused through failure, and choose to see it not as an end point, but merely a point along the greater timeline of innovation, then you're able to take the pressure off and allow the idea to take the time it needs to grow and develop.

Failure is an aspect of everyday life in Silicon Valley.

Probably one of the most unique things about the region is its capacity to celebrate, and to champion, failure. While I encourage all businesses interested in cultivating an innovative workspace to incorporate this ideal into their own approach, I understand the contrast may be quite stark.

We are generally, as humans, not interested in focusing on our failures. Unfortunately, though, what we should really be doing is digging underneath the surface of our failures, to uncover what curiosities and questions lie beneath, waiting to be poked, prodded, uncovered and discovered.

Failure holds a deep well of potential for innovative growth, if only we can get past our holdups and shortcomings and choose to engage with the learning process in this humble way.

In Silicon Valley, failure is honorable. I believe it was Sun Tzu, who wrote, "If you know the enemy and know yourself, you need not fear the result of a hundred battles. If you know yourself but not the enemy, for every victory gained you will also suffer a defeat. If you know neither the enemy nor yourself, you will succumb in every battle."

This only stands to further highlight the potential value of failure, and all that it can offer the creation process and progress. Success and failure are but two cogs in a greater chain called innovation, and you do not need to waste your time getting caught up in failure as a stop sign.

In the Valley, you're more likely to get a raise if your last venture was a flop, than if it was a success. Being a real risk taker (though calculated, still) is of high value here. A revered trait, to be sure.

This isn't without reason. Failure translates to, "someone else paid the tuition for your learning experience so now I don't have to." The saying, here in the Valley, is to "fail fast" so you can move forward. Onward to the next part of the adventure!

No one likes to keep a dead business afloat by the skin of its teeth, so it's far better to fail and get that part out of the way, so you're not cringing to keep the status quo, and can instead walk fearlessly ever forward.

Silicon Valley is a very different market than the US, Europe or Latin America, where I come from, so you play different rules here. Companies come here very early. Available money drives the entire mindset. Action happens much quicker than elsewhere. One of the strengths of the Silicon Valley way is the unique pay-it-forward culture that makes up the bulk of the energy that moves through it.

Don't be disheartened by rejection, no matter where in the world you're running your business from. Reframe your rejections into free consulting that helps you get to the essence of what matters most for your product.

If you want to make any kind of progress, you have to take risks.

As an innovator, you know intuitively when something isn't working. When you do see something wrong, it should be an immediate red flag. Take the risks and move. You will make mistakes. Your job is to fix them as quickly as possible, and innovate them out.

Your job is to fail fast, get up faster, and then to keep on moving forward.

CHAPTER EIGHT

THE LIFELONG SCHOOL OF LEARNING

"Your horse is only as fast as your brain. Every time you learn something, your horse will move ahead."

— Carol Dweck, Stanford

Our world has changed drastically over the course of the past few decades. One of the most major areas which has felt the impact of this rapid change is in our careers.

Careers are changing, across the board, because the companies; the market is changing. The "secure career choice" is a lost entity. An entirely bygone era.

Now, in its place, stands an approach of constant adaptation and reinvention of one's skill set in pursuit of their career. And by constant, I mean continuous, intrepid, ever evolving, and so on. I mean, there is no beginning and no end point to one's "success" in the ways there once were.

Almost everyone is an entrepreneur in some form. If nothing else, a true jack of all trades. Our world now demands it.

In this landscape, how is it that you get ahead? Simple. You must begin to implement a cycle of lifelong learning that will automate the process for you. You must begin to adapt by nature, and get so used to growing and evolving, that it becomes your norm.

When you can implement this Lifelong Learning approach, you will gain an edge over your competitors, and your tactic will be sustainable enough to support not only your career, but the evolution of your *self*, as well: The thing driving your career forward.

Innovation is led by this pursuit of continuously integrating new data. Each and every team member must be of heart and mind to grow and evolve without remorse or attachment to old ideas. Otherwise, your success may be adversely affected, and innovation will be clouded by confusion and conflict amongst team members.

So don't get attached. The shelf life for knowledge is simply shorter now, which means that you absolutely must always be teachable, and ready to explore fresh surroundings with curiosity as your main tool.

This commitment to the School of Lifelong Learning is crucial to your venturial success, and all of Silicon Valley implements it, each in their own way. Some create a morning ritual to scroll through and integrate new data and tools which apply to their niche. Others exercise team meetings around integration and analysis, giving a homework of sorts for each team member to bring to the table.

Learning is something that compounds upon itself, and as you dig in, it'll become easier and easier to implement faster and faster. You will attract the information you need in odd and unexpected ways as you begin to direct your focus acutely.

Adaptation is the result of a curious and willing mind; one which adapts almost without effort, but always through balance. Commit yourself to growth, personally and professionally, and apply whatever steps necessary to bring this commitment to life through action.

In order to develop, a successful company or person will have to constantly evolve in the technologies it uses, in understanding new business models, and in new forms of management and relationship with the market.

Adapting fluidly to change in these ways is now more essential in the workplace than ever before.

When you work for any type of venture in Silicon Valley, things change really fast. I'm talking lightning fast speeds, here. The turnaround is expedient.

No longer do we have any use for those strategic five-year plans. Heck, don't look too far forward; it's an uncalculated risk! Instead, stay alert to the changes and shifts you notice in the present, becoming opportunistic in how you approach your work.

Take the new technologies, new personas, new market, new tools, new ideas, and *integrate*. Take on this high-quality problem, and solve it. Continuously.

And while you do have to change quickly in these modern times, you do not have to do it alone.

Your team, your comrades, even your competition is working to evolve alongside you. Find comfort in that change is the only constant, and where this used to be a philosophical ideal, it is now the physical norm, especially in the fields driven by innovation.

Keep yourself and your team motivated by embracing this truth, that all change emits potential for growth in the direction of success. The direction of dreams realized, of excitement and joy, as the world shifts around you in response to your high growth rate, where things can happen a lot quicker than they used to.

Some things may fall apart, but as I've said before, don't get too attached, and ride these waves of change with a keen eye searching out for solutions to whatever problems arise.

Be sure to utilize the unique strengths of how you and your team members learn, as a means of motivating the integration and commitment to lifelong learning. Suggest different media and sources to different team members, as they align with their unique tastes and interests.

Bring spontaneity into the workplace in response to shifts in the market. Change the way you embrace change, even. Allow innovation to become the lifeblood of your operation, inside and out.

The search, the journey, is all about heart. Your passion fuels this learning, so be sure there is heart in it. Fuse together innovation with your passion to ensure you don't get stuck forcing the momentum. No fun will be had if the effort is futile, or if the change is painful.

Make it fun. Don't — please don't — be afraid to make it fun… and for everyone on your team! The whole journey is a creative exploration, so why not allow it to be as such. Don't let your experiences at poor or low-morale companies or school systems deter you from embracing your natural ability to integrate change and grow in a way that is fun and exciting!

If anything else, it will make your days all go a lot quicker, especially when you want them to, and it will greatly benefit the culture of your workspace.

Each of us is preparing for an unknown future, and all we have to guide us is the current collective. Staying aware of what is happening in your niche field is vital. Remaining vigilant in your focus to what changes benefit, what changes distract, and discerning the value of what to implement with your team with make it or break it.

Solve the problems that call out your passion, and allow the same for your team members. This personal curiosity, learning, integration and implementation process is how the big ideas get generated and where the changemakers originate from.

It won't work — none of this will work — if you wait to see what's changed before you integrate, however. This is one key thing I see many entrepreneurs miss. Do not reactively change; proactively integrate!

To be at the forefront you must actually *be at the forefront* of change. Your key responsibility is to continuously sponge yourself, absorbing and releasing as what does and does not work for you or your venture as need be.

And look! Tech and new tools have made it so much easier to learn and witness the changes in the collective current. So use this! Instead of allowing this ease to cause reactive laziness, use it as leverage to move even faster through the landscape.

Create a lifelong learning style that suits you, and allows you to feel calm and grounded as you quickly and efficiently glide through data as it is revealed.

The current of quickened change is very exciting, but sometimes it is somewhat like watching a train crash. Pace is everything, from keeping up with competitors, to soaring past them without losing touch or burning out.

Find yours, and bring it into the fold.

I, for one, am excited to see where we go.

CHAPTER NINE

NEVER-ENDING CIRCLE

"Tough times bring out the best parts
of Silicon Valley"

— Sergey Brin, Google

Silicon Valley's startup cycle is never-ending. Startup teammates often get rich quickly, only to quit and turn around to become venture capitalists in their next breath.

One brilliant case of this is the Paypal Mafia I brought up earlier. The company that was founded by Elon Musk, Peter Thiel and Max Levchin created three billionaires and several other millionaires, while expounding the careers of every member involved.

The popularized narrative of American innovation is that it is suffering. That public companies run away with their profits after returning them to their shareholders rather than investing them in research, wherein the money gets swept away in expensive and needless materialistic purchases.

However, in Silicon Valley, it's nothing like that. The norm here is as follows:

1. Someone starts a company with venture funding
2. The company gets huge and makes many teammates millionaires, as they are all owners themselves (via chapter five)
3. The teammates all quit to become venture capitalists

4. The money flows out of the startup into the pockets of teammates, who put it right back to work in other startups.

It may seem potentially off-putting to consider how easy it is for some young men and women to turn into venture capitalists so young, thereafter simply investing their money, and their friends' monies, in other people's ventures.

However, from an innovation perspective, it seems like a virtuous cycle.

The ecosystem is balanced, and all are rewarded in surprising ways which make it impossible to settle, fully exit or give up.

How, though, if you do not live in Silicon Valley, can you become a part of this never-ending cycle?

In the end, venture success is about solving the important problems in simple ways.

You can be anywhere in the world to do this. You can be doing and exploring anything, in any location, so long as you remain close to the problem at hand and continuously apply your passion to solving it.

Passion trumps any kind of high profile or position, every time.

The key is in navigating your efforts to align with the most profitable reservoirs of abundant innovation, wherever you can. Wherever you are.

Tech hot spots are starting to crop up all over the world, where you'll see your favorite under-patroned coffee shop now flush with laptops and purveyors galore.

From Boulder to Ibiza, locations are being overtaken by tech and innovation entrepreneurs whose integration into the cycle is in no way geo-location oriented.

Each locale may present its challenges, but so too does Silicon Valley. Here, often the biggest risk to the livelihood of the ecosystem comes via groupthink.

Because of the cyclical nature of this particular locale, the biggest challenge is in bringing consistent innovation to the fore. New ideas are often rare, and when they occur, spread like wildfire amongst various ventures.

Then the competition comes alive, and before you know it, your idea has been implemented by others in ways which make your original fingerprint idea obsolete.

The non-conformists succeed, but their success isn't trackable. Innovation isn't something you can plan for; merely, providing the proper platforms is all you can do to prepare.

These massive groupthinks develop and leave in their wake massive loss. They abandon innovation in support of "what works" and they are eternally in response to what else is occurring within the echo of the groupthink.

This is where there remains potential benefit to existing outside of the ecosystem.

Blossoming companies have more room for growth when their ideas are not gobbled up and hyper-processed right next door. They can expand with a bit less fear of the others, and a bit more natural trust in the flow of the process.

Companies outside the Valley's collective current can still benefit from its financial support, as well as the global web of connection being formed more and more strongly every day.

Sometimes, existing outside this competitive congestion is your team's greatest asset, as it allows you to focus on your goals while gleaning insight from the Valley.

No matter where the team is located; no matter from where an idea originates, it has an equal potential to get funding. Sure, of course it's trickier to get a meeting casually. You must seek it out. But when you do, you are sure to stand out as a viable system in need of valid support.

The capital exists, and it is plenty. Work with what you have to get what you need. The money isn't loyal to the Valley. VCs are often very accommodating to outliers. They like a calculated risk, as much as anyone raised in the Never-Ending Circle.

Wherever in the world you are, reading this, and developing your idea, do remember to contribute to the ecosystem of that locale. In whatever ways you can.

Remember this never-ending cycle of innovation, and let that inspire you to get involved in whatever ways you can, to support the ecosystem that supports you back.

CHAPTER TEN

GIVE BACK

"Although I don't have a prescription for what others should do, I know I have been very fortunate and feel a responsibility to give back to society in a very significant way."

— Bill Gates, Microsoft

The main lesson I have learned from my time spent in Silicon Valley is the powerful impact you make by contributing to the ecosystem you live and work within. When you give, it returns tenfold.

The impact happens when you fall into networks where you can multiply your learning, your business, your leadership, and ultimately, your dream.

Nowadays, our version of small talk is to ask people we casually meet about their current trends and tech followings. We instantly dig into discussion around what projects they're working on, what they do for a living, or what exciting niche developments they've noticed in the field.

Especially in Silicon Valley, the air is filled with sparks of innovation and collaborative-based conversation. Everyone and everything is business, and as such, is up for discussion. The ecosystem is balanced by a continuous array of informal mentorships and fortuitous friendships, popping and cropping up in the most surprising and organic of ways.

I believe this, if anything, is what people don't see clearly as the magic of Silicon Valley. There exists a quintessential sense of camaraderie between everyone who lives here that allows some of the most unexpectedly ingenious collaborations to arise, whether in people, creations, or ideations.

Sure, some of the best minds live here! Why do you think I live here now? But the real secret sauce is the kindness and willingness to support and connect with one another, while continuing to remain competitively ignited.

Sometimes, two strangers will start a company together based on an enticing interaction. Conversation will bleed into collaboration which then bleeds into investing, which bleeds into new ideas, ventures, startups, and breakthroughs.

The Valley is an entire city of made up of creators, cross-examiners, trailblazers, and the best news is, we are very open to sharing.

We understand that ideas do not mean as much as execution. We recognize the honorable value of failure. And most of all, we know firsthand of the vital difference trust can make in any business venture. Trust on both sides. Trust from leadership. And trust from teammates.

And really just a blossoming, cohesive ecosystem of collective trust throughout the region. Whatever your idea, you are bound to find others pointing you in the right direction with a willing hand as you search to find those with whom you can connect.

There's never any shortage of willing, ready, like-minded collaborators.

I believe this distends very much from the collective desire amongst those who find success in the valley to give back to those who've given to them.

There exists this strong air of reciprocity, and that extends further than you can imagine. For thirty years, the energy of this place has been building upon this reciprocity, and I believe that's why you can really feel it in the air.

So, wherever you are and whatever you do, I encourage you to give back to the society that nurtures you. I encourage you to use your same innovative and creative tendencies to — if it doesn't already exist — start the motion for reciprocity the same way you would begin any new venture.

I encourage you to put aside any beliefs that there isn't enough to go around; to put aside any doubts that it will come back, and to give freely, from the creative and alive heart, to those for whom you feel grateful. To those you feel may need nurturing.

Not to even mention the emotional rewards you receive from giving back to your community, there is some sort of magic ripple effect that begins to spread once you make an effort.

So, give.

Give something you treasure, and freely release it!

Lean into this trust exercise and allow this to compound your business and personal efforts without your ever tracking or realizing it!

THE VALLEY WAY

Living in Silicon Valley is not imperative to understanding and integrating its lessons into your venture.

You can start today to implement what I've shared with you in this book. You can start now to develop your business in line with what those in the most successful region of the world are doing.

All you have to do is start with one step at a time.

What is your purpose? Cultivate this and seek out someone who will challenge your way of thinking to push you to develop a cohesive venture design.

Then build your team and develop the culture. This phase will allow you to witness the ecosystem you're creating. It may feel like an overwhelming and life-or-death time of the business cycle, so don't forget to let it breathe as much as you can.

I suggest to you to ensure your mindset is in the right place, and that you encourage yourself to indulge equally as to the benefits you offer the team members you bring on board.

This will encourage your own ownership mentality to remain grounded and stable as you work to support that of your teammates. As well, will diverse thinking and creative play allow your team to naturally grow and develop in innovative directions as the ecosystem gets stronger and stronger.

As you begin to implement your ideas, you must push past the ideation phase and dig your heels deep into the process of execution. Execute with intensity, every time, and don't be afraid to fail.

Failure is a true badge of honor here in the Valley, so when you do fail, do so quickly, and get right back up again to keep moving brazenly towards your goals.

And be sure to learn from your failures! While you're at it, work to establish a pattern of growth, wherein you can effortlessly be in a continuous state of perpetual learning, as you develop and grow your startup, business, or venture.

Last but most certainly not least, engage with your larger ecosystem. Support the cycle of innovation by getting involved in the cycle as it occurs in your area.

Give back to the environment; the society you work within, to nourish it to grow, which will in turn nourish your business to continue to flourish, getting brighter and brighter as it comes into the view of the rest of the world.

I sincerely hope you take away these messages with you when you close this book. I know these lessons are useful, as I have applied, as well as supported others in applying these same ideals and techniques to their own ventures, with many desired results.

Though it may not be easy to implement some of these shifts the Silicon Valley way, it will pay off to begin now. Digging in. As deeply as I have to find the successes of which you already know you are capable.

To find those successes, and innovate even more so, to then share with the next set of innovators who seek venture growth for themselves!

Thank you for joining me on this journey.

I wish you the best of luck on yours!

REFERENCES

Chapter One :
[1] Saggese, Chelsea. "Purpose: The Secret Ingredient to Startup Success." Interbrand, 2019, www.interbrand.com/views/purpose-the-secret-ingredient-to-startup-success/.

[2] Matveeva, Sophia. "What Makes Great Startup Teams, And How To Find It." Forbes, Forbes Magazine, 30 Apr. 2018, www.forbes.com/sites/sophiamatveeva/2018/04/30/what-makes-great-start-up-teams-and-how-to-find-it/#3c449b6216f6.

Chapter Four :
[1] Zwilling, Martin. "7 Ways to Incent Employees to Feel and Act as Owners." Inc.com, Inc., 16 Feb. 2018, www.inc.com/martin-zwilling/7-ways-to-incent-employees-to-feel-act-as-owners.html.

Chapter Five :
[1] and [2] Folz, Christina. "Adam Grant Explains How to Unleash Originality in Your Organization." SHRM, SHRM, 16 Aug. 2019, www.shrm.org/hr-today/news/hr-news/conference-today/pages/2018/adam-grant-unleash-originality-in-your-organization.aspx.

ABOUT THE AUTHOR

Passionate about technology, innovation and entrepreneurship, Felipe has a degree in Computing (Pontifical Catholic University of Minas Gerais), an MBA in Project Management (FGV) in Brazil and a Project Management Professional Certification by PMI Institute. In addition, he holds a degree in Marketing and Global Business from UC Berkeley — one of the top three universities in the world — and a master's degree in Computing from the International Technological University in San Jose, Silicon Valley.

With a nearly 15-year career in technology, much of that time was spent playing key roles at TOTVS, whereafter Felipe decided to resign and give up a structured career at Latin America's largest software company to move to Silicon Valley, the most innovative ecosystem on the planet. In 2017, he was awarded by Entrepreneur Juscelino Kubitschek the Cross of Merit, and was recognized as Entrepreneur of the Year at the Brazilian National Congress.

A member of the StartSe (lifelong learning company) team since 2016, Felipe is a partner and one of the creators, mentors, and organizers of Silicon Valley immersion programs teaching executives, entrepreneurs, and investors from around the world the teachings presented in this book.